# Withdrawn

W9-DGV-937

EXTREME WINTER
SPORTS ZONE

# SKI SUPERPIPE

*Darice Bailer*

ᴸ Lerner Publications Company • Minneapolis

Lerner Publications Company
A division of Lerner Publishing Group, Inc.
241 First Avenue North
Minneapolis, MN 55401 U.S.A.

Website address: www.lernerbooks.com

Content Consultant: Skogen Sprang, freeskiing pioneer, X Games medalist, and current U.S. Freeskiing Slopestyle Team coach

With special thanks to Canadian Half-Pipe Team Head Coach Trennon Paynter, U.S. freeskiers Devin Logan and Peter Olenick, and Justine Spence, the U.S. Freeskiing press officer, for all of their help.

Library of Congress Cataloging-in-Publication Data

Bailer, Darice.
    Ski superpipe / by Darice Bailer.
       pages    cm. — (Extreme winter sports zone)
    Includes index.
    ISBN 978–1–4677–0757–2 (lib. bdg. : alk. paper)
    ISBN 978–1–4677–1732–8 (eBook)
    1. Skis and skiing—Juvenile literature.  2. Extreme sports—Juvenile literature.  I. Title
GV854.315.B36  2014
796.93—dc23                                                          2013001739

Manufactured in the United States of America
1—PP—7/15/13

The images in this book are used with the permission of: © Jonathan Moore/Getty Images, 5; Haslam Photography/Shutterstock Images, 6, 11, 14, 27; Christian Murdock/The Colorado Springs Gazette/AP Images, 7; AP Images, 8; Kevin Zen/Getty Images, 9; Jeffrey Van Daele/Shutterstock Images, 10; Vincent Curutchet/DPPI/Icon SMI, 12, 28; Donald Miralle/Getty Images, 13; Vincent Curutchet/DPPI/Icon SMI, 15; Aaron Ontiveroz/The Denver Post/AP Images, 16; Nathan Bilow/AP Images, 17, 20; Doug Pensinger/Getty Images, 18, 19; Richard Bord/Getty Images, 21; Ryan Slabaugh/The Aspen Times/AP Images, 22-23; Rick Bowmer/AP Images, 24; Nick Stubbs/Shutterstock Images, 25; gorillaimages/Shutterstock Images, 26; Aurelien Meunier/Icon SMI, 28, 29; Marc Piscotty/Icon SMI, 29.

Front cover: © Doug Pensinger/Getty Images; backgrounds: © kcv/Shutterstock.com.

Main body text set in Folio Std Light 11/17.
Typeface provided by Adobe Systems.

# TABLE OF CONTENTS

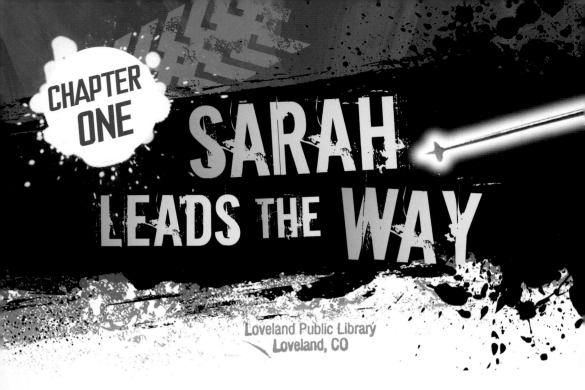

# CHAPTER ONE

# SARAH LEADS THE WAY

Sarah Burke smiled at the top of the snowy ramp. It was January 27, 2011. Burke was heading into her second run of the ski superpipe finals at the Winter X Games in Aspen, Colorado. The Winter X Games is one of the most exciting extreme sports competitions of the year. Athletes compete for medals and prize money. Before pushing off, Burke high-fived her coach. In moments, Burke would be performing aerial spins and flips off the superpipe, a U-shaped ditch with 22-foot (6.7-meter) walls.

Burke was 28 years old. She had been skiing since she was just five years old. This was her seventh trip to the Winter X Games. She had won three gold medals and two silver medals in past superpipe competitions. But this year, a medal seemed like a long shot for Burke. She was recovering from shoulder surgery. She'd had only nine days to practice before the 2011 Winter X Games. And Burke hadn't skied her best during the elimination rounds the night before. She was in last place going into the finals. To make matters worse, she had fallen on her first of the three finals runs.

Sarah Burke won her third gold medal in superpipe at the 2009 Winter X Games in Aspen, Colorado.

One of the things that made Burke so successful was her ability to shake off a fall and keep going. She did just that on her second run. Burke skied up the left wall of the pipe and shot into the frosty night sky. Then she landed, skied down the wall back into the pipe, and soared up the other side. She flipped head over heels high in the air, spinning around like a corkscrew. Burke spun around two and a half times. It was a 900-degree spin, or a 900. Many of Burke's competitors could spin a 900 upright. But Burke did it the hard way, with her body upside down.

## NEVER GIVE UP

Burke had always dreamed of winning a medal in the Olympic Games. But ski superpipe was not an Olympic event. Burke helped convince the International Olympic Committee (IOC) to add the sport to the 2014 Olympic Games in Sochi, Russia. Sadly, Burke died before she could compete in the Olympic Games. In 2012 she fell during a practice run and damaged her brain. The accident was a reminder about how dangerous ski superpipe can be. Because of her efforts to bring her sport to the Olympic Games, Burke was inducted into the Canadian Olympic Hall of Fame alongside Canada's greatest Olympians.

Burke stomped the landing. Then she shot up the snow-packed wall and began a backflip. She twisted halfway around so she could ski down the wall facing forward after her flip. The trick is called a flair. Then Burke raced up the other side of the pipe and performed a mirror image of the trick. On her last trick, Burke skied up the pipe and twirled around upside down. Then she tilted to one side, in a cork 720 (two rotations). *Cork* means "an off-axis rotation." She landed backward and continued skiing into the bottom of the pipe as she ended her run.

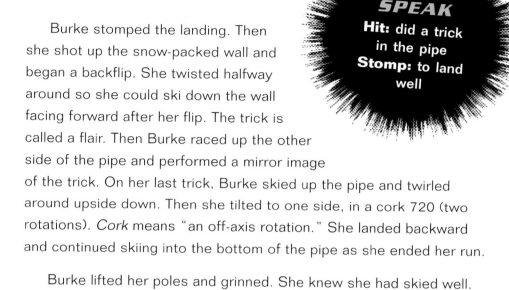

**SKI SPEAK**

**Hit:** did a trick in the pipe
**Stomp:** to land well

Burke lifted her poles and grinned. She knew she had skied well. Her score just might be high enough to win. "She did it!" someone in the crowd yelled. The judges announced her score: 91.33. It was the highest score of the night. The score earned Burke her fourth Winter X Games gold medal. She was a superpipe hero.

Skier Kim Lamarre wears a helmet honoring Burke. Burke's death shook the freestyle skiing community.

7

# CHAPTER TWO

# THE PIPE AND ITS BEGINNINGS

Jason Levinthal liked to skateboard up steep ramps. He liked to race up half-pipes on his snowboard and catch air. He liked to do exciting tricks in the water on his wakeboard. But Levinthal liked downhill skiing best. He wanted to catch air and do awesome tricks on skis. He had just one problem. He didn't have a pair of skis that worked like the boards he used in other action sports.

Traditional downhill skis curved up in the front and were flat in the back.

Ancient skiers in the Altai Mountains of China likely used horsehair-covered skis similar to these. A few craftsmen still make these skis.

Downhill skis have front tips that curve up and flat tails. The curved tip allowed Levinthal to ski forward up the wall of a half-pipe. But if he skied backward, the tails would dig into the snow. Levinthal would crash.

## ANCIENT SKIERS

Ski superpipe is a new sport. But humans have been skiing for thousands of years. Some historians believe that early Europeans called Cro-Magnons used skis as much as 22,000 years ago. Cro-Magnons probably used these early skis to travel and hunt. Early humans may have even used skis before they created the wheel. The earliest known skis were discovered in Russia. These are probably more than 7,000 years old!

Snowboards are shorter and wider than skis and have two curved tips. Levinthal hoped skis with similar features would allow him to do some of the stunning tricks snowboarders could do.

## A New Kind of Ski

In 1995 when Levinthal was 21, he needed to design something for a college project. He decided to make a new kind of ski. Levinthal used the school woodshop to build a pair of skis. These skis were designed to handle the half-pipe. The skis curved up in the front, like normal skis. But they also curved up in back, similar to skateboards and snowboards. Levinthal's new skis were twice the width and half the length of normal skis. Levinthal called his invention skiboards.

When Levinthal finished making his skiboards, he tested them. He could ski backward and do tricks he could never pull off on regular skis. Levinthal decided to start his own company to make and sell his skiboards. Levinthal called his new company Line Skis. Before long Levinthal was getting orders for as many as a thousand pairs of skiboards at a time.

Three years later, a company named Salomon began selling twin-tip skis. These were longer than Levinthal's skiboards. Salomon's twin-tip ski was called the Teneighty. Skiers were ready to take their sport to the next level. Twin-tips were perfect for skiers who wanted to ski like snowboarders. This type of skiing is known as freeskiing. Some freeskiers use jumps and rails to do tricks. This is known as slopestyle skiing. Other freeskiers focus on doing tricks in the half-pipe.

The twin tips on superpipe skier Anais Caradeux's skis allow her to ski forward and backward in the pipe.

Kevin Rolland soars off the 22-foot (6.7 m) superpipe at the 2010 European Winter X Games in Tignes, France.

## Half-Pipes Become Superpipes

Freeskiers started doing tricks on half-pipes that were usually 11 feet 6 inches (3.5 m) tall. As freeskiers learned bigger and better tricks, the half-pipe grew. By the time ESPN added the sport to the 2002 Winter X Games, freeskiers were using a superpipe. A superpipe is a giant half-pipe ramp with walls that are at least 18 feet (5.4 m) tall. In 2008 some superpipes grew to 22 feet (6.7 m) high. That's as tall as a two-story building. All professional freeskiing half-pipe competitions use the 22-foot superpipe. But not all competitions changed the name as the Winter X Games did. Many competitions, such as the Olympic Games, still call the event half-pipe.

Candide Thovex wowed spectators with his daring moves and amazing height. His tricks won him the gold medal in men's superpipe at the 2003 Winter X Games.

## SKIING THROUGH TIME

- **6300–5000 B.C.:** The oldest skis ever discovered were created in Russia.

- **A.D. 1841:** The first skier is reported in the United States.

- **1995:** Jason Levinthal makes a pair of twin-tip skis in college.

- **1998:** Salomon begins selling its own twin-tip ski, called the Teneighty.

- **2002:** Men's ski superpipe debuts at the Winter X Games.

- **2005:** Women's ski superpipe is added to Winter X Games.

- **2011:** Men's and women's ski superpipe competitions are added to the 2014 Winter Olympic Games in Sochi, Russia.

Ski superpipe was still young when it was added to the 2002 Winter X Games. Not many people knew about the sport. That changed at the 2003 Winter X Games. A Frenchman named Candide Thovex grabbed the world's attention. He threw down 900s and an inverted (upside-down) 720. Thovex rocketed 20 feet (6 m) above the pipe. No one had ever seen a skier catch that much air in the pipe before. Thovex brought attention to ski superpipe. He showed the world that whether you call it a half-pipe or a superpipe, the sport is anything but dull.

# CHAPTER THREE

# SKIING THE SUPERPIPE

In 2011 the IOC announced that ski superpipe would become an Olympic sport in 2014. The U.S. Ski and Snowboard Association (USSA) put together a pro U.S. Freeskiing Half-Pipe Team. If the team's skiers are good enough, the United States will send four men and four women to Sochi, Russia, in 2014. The USSA also formed a U.S. Freeskiing Rookie Team. This team features talented teenage skiers. They could move up to the pros if they perform well at national competitions.

Superpipe star Jen Hudak skis at the 2010 Dew Tour. Hudak is a member of the U.S. Freeskiing Half-Pipe Team.

A superpipe-shaping machine works on the 2010 Winter X Games Europe superpipe.

The U.S. Freeskiing Pro Team trains at the Center of Excellence in Park City, Utah. The teams also train on Copper Mountain, in Colorado. Ski superpipe is a dangerous sport. Many athletes are injured. Some are even killed attempting risky tricks. Superpipe athletes learn new tricks safely by practicing before trying them in the pipe. Superpipe skiers practice flips on indoor trampolines. They use artificial snow and indoor ski ramps to practice tricks safely year-round. On these ramps, pros ski down a surface covered in white plastic bristles. Then they land in huge wooden pits filled with foam blocks. Once skiers feel they have mastered a trick, they can then go outside and stomp it in the snow.

## MAKING A PIPE

Making a superpipe takes a lot of hard work. It takes a lot of water to make the amount of snow that is needed. Wet snow works better than dry, powdery snow because wet snow packs and sticks together more easily. Workers use a big machine that looks like a bulldozer to push the snow into a pile and dig out the pipe.

David Wise soared his way to a gold medal in ski superpipe at the 2013 Winter X Games.

## The Competitions

Ski superpipe is now an Olympic event. But the Winter X Games is still one of the biggest superpipe competitions in the world. The best skiers from around the globe show up to compete each January. As many as 12,000 spectators cheer the skiers on. The competition is broadcast live on television around the world. Two months later, many of the same athletes fly to France for the Winter X Games Europe in Tignes, France.

### SKIERS ON-SCREEN

Freeskiers don't just do rad tricks on skis. They also make movies! Winter X Games gold medalist Jen Hudak starred in the Ski Channel film *Winter*, which aired in 2011. She also helped create a three-part webisode series called "Moving Mountains," which is available online. In the series, Hudak talks about her training. She tells viewers what it's like to compete at the Winter X Games. She also discusses the challenges she faces as a professional skier.

The Winter and European X Games are just two of many events that make up the Association of Freeskiing Professionals (AFP) World Tour. Each skier won't compete at all events. But athletes earn points toward the AFP World Ranking for every AFP competition they participate in.

The North American ski season usually lasts from November to late April. One of the first contests of the season is the Winter Dew Tour. After that is the Sprint U.S. Grand Prix tour. Skiers can also compete in the International Ski Federation (FIS) World Cup. The FIS holds World Cup superpipe competitions in the United States, Russia, Spain, and other countries.

The Sprint U.S. Grand Prix and the World Cups feature qualifying events for the Olympic Games. Skiers who perform well may land a spot on the U.S. Freeskiing Half-Pipe Team.

Belgium's Nicolas Elshout competes at a 2011 FIS World Cup competition in Park City, Utah.

## Scoring Superpipe

Judges score superpipe skiers' runs. Superpipe skiers usually perform five or six tricks during a run. Most competitions have five judges scoring the skiers. The judges look at execution, or how well the skiers take off and land their tricks. Superpipe judges also consider the difficulty, variety, and amplitude (height) of the tricks. They watch for how smoothly the athletes move from trick to trick. Then the five judges award scores from 1 to 100. In the Winter X Games, each athlete gets three runs. Other events give athletes two runs. Each run is scored separately. The highest score counts as the skier's final score.

## FREESTYLE FIRSTS

- At the 2010 Winter X Games superpipe star Peter Olenick shot 24 feet 11 inches (7.6 m) into the air. He landed in the Guinness Book of World Records for the highest air in a superpipe.

- In 2011 Torin Yater-Wallace was the youngest skier ever to medal at the Winter X Games. He was just 15 years old when he won the silver medal in ski superpipe.

- Superpipe gold medalist Grete Eliassen holds the record for the highest hip jump (similar to a half-pipe with a steep angle at the top). In 2010 she skied up a 30-foot (9.1 m) hip jump and soared more than 31 feet (9.4 m) high.

- In 2012 Brita Sigourney became the first woman to land a 1080 spin in a superpipe.

Torin Yater-Wallace soars above the superpipe at the 2011 Winter X Games.

# CHAPTER FOUR
# HITTING THE SNOW

**B**ecoming a superpipe pro is a lot of work. It means many hours of training and countless hard falls. It's very dangerous to drop into a pipe without any training. The pipe is icy. Even pros get badly hurt. Some, like Burke, have died.

**SKI SPEAK**
**Sick:** something amazing
**Grommet:** a young skier

Even pros such as Jen Hudak crash on the superpipe.

Superpipe skiers must use proper safety gear. But safety gear can only protect a skier so much. It can't fully protect someone who crashes racing 30 miles (48 kilometers) per hour. Because of the dangers, superpipe skiers need to be very careful. Pro superpipe skiers work with experienced coaches. Athletes know not to try tricks beyond their abilities. And they practice new tricks off the snow before taking them to the pipe.

# GREAT SUPERPIPE GEAR

## SKIS

Twin-tip skis for superpipe shouldn't bend too easily. Enough stiffness makes it easier for the skis' edges to turn on the icy pipe wall. A trained salesperson at a local ski shop can help a new skier find just the right ones. The ski size is based on a skier's height and weight.

## BOOTS

Boots cushion the landing after a trick. Boots need to keep a skier's ankles stable. Good boots should be stiff and snug but comfortable. Superpipe boots are light so skiers can easily move around.

Canada's Roz Groenewoud wears the right superpipe safety gear at the 2012 Winter X Games.

## HELMET

All skiers fall sometimes. Ski helmets save lives and help protect skiers from serious brain injuries. A helmet also keeps a skier's head warm. A good helmet is hard on the outside with padding on the inside. It should feel snug on the head but still fit comfortably.

## GOGGLES

Bright sun can bounce off a patch of snow, making it hard to see. A good pair of goggles shields eyes from the sun's damaging rays. Goggles also protect a skier's eyes from wind and snow. Ski goggles should have tough lenses that won't scratch or shatter during a fall.

## PADS

Skiers in the superpipe need body protection. Most athletes wear padded shorts or pants under ski pants. These help protect a skier's hips, knees, backside, and tailbone. Upper-body padded tops and forearm or elbow pads also cushion a fall.

Windells camp in Oregon features indoor trampolines and foam pits where superpipe skiers and snowboarders can safely practice tricks before trying them in the snow.

## Becoming a Superpipe Star

Becoming a pro superpipe skier takes a lot of hard work. A gymnastics class can help skiers learn how to somersault in the air. Ski camps also teach young skiers the skills they need to eventually tackle the superpipe. At some camps, pro skiers even help teach rookies to ski safely.

It's important for someone who wants to try skiing in the pipe to master basic ski skills first. All skiers need to know how to slow down, stop, and turn on skis. Beginners can practice carving turns down a mountain. Doing this helps new skiers learn balance. They also learn how to control the edges of their skis.

Rookie skiers can try skiing in a small half-pipe once they're comfortable on regular downhill ski trails.

Downhill skiing is a fun activity and a great way to get outside in the winter.

Becoming a ski superpipe pro like U.S. freeskier Kristi Leskinen takes a lot of practice.

## Practice, Practice, Practice

Pros pop off the pipe, spin high in the air, and land their tricks. Young skiers might not be ready to pull off the same stunning moves in the superpipe. But superpipe hopefuls can practice the skills they might one day need. One important move is a 180-degree spin. Try standing in one place on a flat patch of snow. Keep your skis straight beneath you. Looking back over your shoulder, jump up off the snow. Use your ankles, knees, and hips to get your skis high off the ground. Keep your hands and poles out in front of you. Look over your shoulder to spot the landing. Unwind toward the spot. Flex your ankles and bend your knees to cushion the landing. Are you facing the opposite way now? If so, you've landed your first trick!

### SUPERPIPE TIPS

Staying balanced and spotting the landing are two of the most important things for superpipe stars to remember. Pros recommend the following tips for new skiers:

- Keep hips over the feet and the middle of the skis.
- Bend at the waist and the knees.
- Hold arms out front and slightly to the side. Poles should be pointed backward.
- Keep the head up and eyes forward.

# SUPERPIPE STARS

## JEN HUDAK

Jen Hudak started skiing in her Vermont backyard when she was just three years old. Hudak began skiing in the half-pipe when she was in high school. She fell in love with the sport. Hudak won bronze medals in superpipe at the Winter X Games in 2007 and 2008. In 2009 she took silver. Then, in 2010, she struck gold, winning the superpipe competition in both the Winter X Games and the Winter X Games Europe. In 2009 and 2010 Hudak was the top ranked female in the world for superpipe.

## DEVIN LOGAN

U.S. freeskier Devin Logan began skiing at the age of two. In addition to being a star in the superpipe, Logan is also a talented slopestyle skier. Logan is one of very few women to compete in both events. She earned the number one spot in the AFP Women's Overall Ranking in both 2011 and 2012. Logan also won the superpipe competition in the 2012 Dew Tour. In 2012 Logan won the Sarah Burke Trophy, the most prestigious award in skiing. The AFP gives the award to the man and the woman with the best overall freeskiing performances in the world.

## DAVID WISE

David Wise began skiing at the age of three. He entered his first half-pipe competition at the age of 12. Wise won four U.S. Championships in a row from 2006 to 2009. Over the 2010–2011 season, Wise became the first person ever to land a double cork 1260 (three and a half rotations) in the superpipe. In 2011 he made the first U.S. Freeskiing Team. Wise went on to win gold medals in superpipe at the 2012 and 2013 Winter X Games.

## TORIN YATER-WALLACE

When Torin Yater-Wallace was just one and a half years old, his mother tied a harness on him. Then she skied, towing her small son behind her. It was the beginning of an exciting career. In 2012 Yater-Wallace was the AFP Men's Half-Pipe World Champion. This meant he was the top-ranked superpipe skier in the world. In 2012 he won the bronze medal at the Winter X Games and the gold medal at the Winter X Games Europe. In 2011 and 2013, Yater-Wallace won silver medals in superpipe at the Winter X Games.

# GLOSSARY

**AERIAL**

in the air

**AIR**

when a skier leaves the ground

**AMPLITUDE**

the height a skier soars during a trick

**FREESKIING**

a type of skiing that combines skiing with flips, twists, and other tricks

**HALF-PIPE**

a snowy ramp that looks like half the inside of a pipe

**PROFESSIONAL**

someone who participates in an activity as a job for payment

**ROOKIE**

someone who is new to a sport or activity

**RUN**

a set of tricks

**SUPERPIPE**

a half-pipe with 22-foot (6.7 m) walls

# FOR MORE INFORMATION

## Further Reading

Bailer, Darice. *Ski Slopestyle*. Minneapolis: Lerner Publications Company, 2014.

Burns, Kylie. *Alpine and Freestyle Skiing*. New York: Crabtree Publishing, 2010.

Hudak, Heather. *Extreme Skiing*. New York: Weigl Publishers, 2009.

## Websites

### Association of Freeskiing Professionals
http://afpworldtour.com/afp10/

The official website for the Association of Freeskiing Professionals (AFP) has the latest superpipe news, rankings, and information about the AFP World Tour.

### Freeskier
http://www.freeskier.com

Check out the cool photos, videos, and interviews with superpipe stars.

### U.S. Freeskiing Team
http://usfreeskiing.com/freeskiing

Learn about the U.S. Ski and Snowboard Association developmental programs for young skiers, and read biographies of the U.S. Freeskiing Team stars.

# INDEX

## *About the Author*

Darice Bailer has written many books for children. She won the Parents' Choice Gold Award for her first book, *Puffin's Homecoming.* She began her career as a sports reporter and is especially fond of writing about sports for kids. She lives in Connecticut with her husband.